GW00707918

contents

the Greensand Way

Stride out along 108 miles of the Greensand Way and discover some of the finest walking experiences in the South East.

The Greensand Way, a joint initiative between Kent County Council and Surrey County Council, has evolved over more than 20 years to offer outstanding experiences to long distance walkers tackling the whole route from Haslemere, in Surrey, through to Hamstreet, in Kent. There are also many opportunities for everyone wishing to sample shorter sections in the two counties.

The route takes in two Areas of Outstanding Natural Beauty – the Surrey Hills and the Kent Downs – as well as numerous Sites of Special Scientific Interest.

In Surrey, the route passes by the highest point in South East England, Leith Hill, through farms and villages along the Greensand Ridge into Kent coming to an end on the now landlocked former cliffs overlooking the haunting levels of Romney Marsh.

This guidebook provides an overview of the many walking opportunities to be enjoyed along the Greensand Way ranging from breathtaking panoramic views to peaceful strolls through valleys, fields and remote farmsteads.

Much of the route passes through ancient and semi-mature woodland ensuring bluebell walks in Spring, cool shade in the height of Summer and amazing displays of colour in Autumn.

Many villages along the way provide a warm and friendly welcome with the chance to rest weary legs, while the peaceful hilltops and inspiring views offer perfect refreshment for the mind.

This guide includes a selection of six short circular walks, ideal for a day out with friends and family, to sample the many and varied delights along the Greensand Way in Kent.

> *"…as for orchards of aples, and gardeins of cherries, and those of the most exquisite and delicious kindes that can be, no part of the Realme (that I know) ….and planted…"*

William Lambarde 1570 who wrote the first history of Kent

Lamberhurst

sands of time

The Greensand Way is named after the sandstone ridge, which crosses Hampshire, Surrey and Kent – one of a series of ridges running west to east across South East England.

These sandstone ridges are the remnants of the great Wealden dome. Compressed layers of marine deposits folded and lifted high above sea level some 10 to 20 million years ago.

Softer bands of chalk, which once formed part of the dome, have been eroded leaving outcrops of upper and lower greensands and, in parts of Kent, outcrops of red sandstone. Beyond the sandstone ridges lie the more resilient chalks of the North and South Downs.

Today the Greensand Ridge scarp rises steeply in Surrey at Gibbet Hill and then flattens before re-emerging east of Nutfield to run eastwards, with a break for the Medway gap, as far as Pluckley. From here, the ground levels drop away sharply above Romney Marsh.

The olive-green tinge to the greensands is due to various amounts of glauconite, an iron-rich silicate. This mineral is a common ingredient in garden fertilisers.

To the east, in the Maidstone area, where the sandstone has a higher lime content giving a blue-grey tinge, it is known as ragstone.

The quality of the sandstone, and associated sands and gravel, for building works is reflected in centuries of quarrying in both Surrey and Kent. Deposits containing Fullers Earth, found between layers of sandstone, have been much sought after near Reigate and Maidstone.

Ide Hill

nature and nurture

The origins of the name of the Weald lie in the Germanic word Wald, meaning woodland. Birch, willow, Scots pine, hazel, oak and elm were among the very early species to become established in the area.

Over the centuries people felled the timber to create grazing and arable land as well as to take advantage of sand and stone near the surface. In sandier areas clearance and grazing depleted the shallow soils. Heathlands were already being created by the Bronze Age.

As agriculture developed, farmers took advantage of richer loamy soils to establish their crops and cultivate fruits. Areas of heavier soils, which retained moisture, provided good pasture. Farming intensified from around the 16th century.

In Surrey, with generally more depleted soils, cattle and pigs predominated with most arable and fruit production in the Vale of Holmsdale.

In the 19th century general cereal production provided an important income but more recently farmers have concentrated on maize, oilseed rape and linseed.

Hops were introduced in the 15th century and hop gardens were established in Kent and in the Farnham area of Surrey. Many oast houses, where the hops were dried, have now been converted into homes.

Heathlands in the more acidic areas in the west of Surrey such as Reigate Heath and Hothfield Common are dominated by ling heather (Calluna vulgaris) with patches of bell heather (Erica cinerea). Where grazing has ceased the heath has become home to secondary woodland with many trees including birch, pendunculate oak and Scots pine. Here bluebells, wood sage and wood sorrel blossom.

While invertebrates flourish on the heathlands, fish and birds thrive in the flooded former sand and stone quarries as well as along the courses of the rivers and streams.

Today much is being done to preserve the landscape and wildlife habitats along the Greensand Way.

Hindhead Commons and the Devil's Punch Bowl cover some 647 hectares (1,600 acres). They are popular destinations for people wishing to savour the splendour of undeveloped countryside.

Grazing of the heathland by commoners ended early in the 20th century allowing the spread of birch, pine and bracken over the heather. There are also fine areas of older woods and wood pasture of oak, holly, ash and beech coppice.

The National Trust is responsible for the care of Toys Hill – 81 hectares (200 acres) of woodland designated as a Site of Special Scientific Interest due to its abundant wildlife.

The Westerham Commons, Hosey and Crockham Hill, are all listed as Sites of Special Scientific Interest. Of particular note are the old ragstone mines which now serve as a hibernation area for five species of bat and are managed as a nature reserve.

Conservation groups look after many other special areas along the Greensand Way including delightful Yalding Fen and Hothfield Common. The latter, another Site of Special Scientific Interest, contains the county's last four valley bogs and one of its last remaining fragments of open heath.

Many plants such as heather, cross-leaved heath, dwarf and common gorse, heath spotted-orchid, bog asphodel, and round-leaved sundew are now thriving, along with keeled skimmer dragonfly and tree pipit as a result of heath and bog habitat restoration.

Work is also being undertaken on the South Willesborough Dykes, a Local Wildlife Site west of the East Stour river. This traditional sheep grazing area in the river's floodplain has been drained by dykes many of which are dry in summer. The wealth of wetland species here includes great crested newts.

Meanwhile, Natural England preserves the environment at Hamstreet National Nature Reserve where the woods are part of the Orlestone Forest which once covered the Weald.

At Hamstreet the key trees are pedunculate and sessile oaks, downy and silver birches, and hornbeam. Bluebells, honeysuckle and wood anemone are found with gorse, ling and tormentil. Damper woodland areas are home to ash, hazel, hawthorn and alder with dogs mercury, greater butterfly and early purple orchid.

Many breeding birds can be seen in the reserve. These include treecreeper, spotted flycatcher and redpoll, nightingale, hawfinch and sparrowhawk.

living landscapes

Evidence of our prehistoric ancestors are plentiful in Kent and Surrey, ranging from the Neolithic Medway Megaliths and long barrows at Reigate Heath to the Iron Age fortifications identified at such sites as Hascombe Hill and Pitch Hill in Surrey, Squerryes Camp above Westerham, and Oldbury north of Ightham in Kent.

The Romans too left their mark on the landscape with routes through the Weald and the lives of Saxons are clearly commemorated within the establishment of many of the villages right along the Greensand Way.

However the hallmark of this route is the number of magnificent houses, gardens and parks, which have been built along the greensand ridge attracting some of the finest architects, interior and landscape designers of their eras.

Many of these properties, built and rebuilt over the years, have been financed by wealth earned by businesses trading in London and overseas. Their owners have been seeking peace and quiet for their families away from the hustle and bustle of city life or opting for a peaceful retirement.

And they have expressed their commitment to enhancing the landcape with fine plantings of specimen trees in their parklands and careful management of their farms and cottages.

Pluckley

In Surrey

Haslemere Educational Museum was founded in 1888 by Sir Jonathan Hutchinson, a distinguished surgeon at the London Hospital. The oldest part of the High Street building dates from the 16th century and, despite alterations in the Victorian era, the façade is clearly Georgian. The gardens contain unusual plants and trees and offer excellent views.

Sandhills and the cottages to be discovered in the picturesque countryside and peaceful village were a key source of inspiration for the watercolourist Helen Allingham. She moved to Sandhills in the 1880s and was moved to paint the landscape and its buildings not only for their artistic value but also for the historical record.

Oakhurst Cottage, at Hambledon, is conserved by The National Trust. The small 16th century timber-framed cottage has been restored and furnished as a simple labourer's dwelling. The interiors include collections from the past four centuries – incorporating part of Gertrude Jekyll's West Surrey Bygones – and the gardens are filled with Victorian plants.

Leith Hill is considered to be one of the highest points in south east England. When it was surveyed in the mid-18th century, members of the Royal Engineers claimed to be able to see 41 London churches from the hilltop. In the 17th century, Richard Hull gained permission to build a prospect tower based on a 14th century Wealden design. Hull and his friends used the tower to view the countryside of the North and South Downs with telescopes. At his request, Hull was buried under the floor of the fortified folly. The Gothic tower, now restored, and the Leith Hill

Box Hill

estate are owned and managed by the National Trust. On a clear day it is possible to see 13 counties from the hill. Leith Hill Place was home to the composer Ralph Vaughan Williams who launched the annual Leith Hill Music Festival.

The **Nower and The Glory Woods** are popular destinations for walkers and local residents. The Nower is a stretch of sandy healthland and woodland given to Dorking by Lt Col R W Barclay in 1932. Today it is conserved for its landscape and ecological value. The Glory Woods was a favourite resort in the late 19th century.

Box Hill, cared for by the National Trust, features in Jane Austen's 1816 novel Emma where the heroine visits the site to find out what "… everybody found so much worth seeing." Box has grown luxuriantly on this site since the 1500s and is much prized as a close-grained wood. More than a dozen species of orchid have been identified on the downland. The River Mole below the escarpment features swallow holes on the limestone and provides an excellent habitat for kingfishers, grey wagtails, moorhens, mandarin ducks and the more recently arrived ring-necked parakeets.

Betchworth Castle was originally an earthwork fortress. A stone castle overlooking the River

Mole was built in the late 14th century. Three hundred years later it was expanded and converted into a sandstone residence by William Fenwick. Much of the masonry was removed from the house in the 19th century.

Reigate Heath Mill is believed to be the only windmill in the world to be used as a place of worship. A post mill was built on the site around 1765. In 1880 the brick roundhouse of the disused mill was turned into a chapel of ease to St Mary's Parish Church, Reigate. Services are held at the former mill throughout the Summer.

Nutfield Priory, now a country hotel, is clearly visible from the Greensand Way and has excellent views over the Surrey and Sussex countryside. The original mansion was built in the 19th century and the current buildings were designed by the architect John Gibson.

Leigh Mill, at Godstone, was recorded as a corn mill in the Domesday Book and was abandoned when the Black Death claimed the lives of local millers. In the 17th century the mill was used for manufacturing gunpowder. The present brick and weatherboard building dates from the 18th century. Leigh Place Pond is thought to be more than 1,500 years old.

East Farleigh

In Kent

Quebec House, just off the Greensand Way link route to Westerham, is conserved by the National Trust. The 17th century red brick gabled house was the childhood home of General James Wolfe who made his name at the Battle of Quebec. Meanwhile the same link route passes Squerryes Court. (Walk 1)

Squerryes Court is a 17th century manor house, which has been the Warde family home since 1731. It is surrounded by 20 acres of attractive and historic gardens which include a lake, restored parterres and an 18th century dovecote. The house and gardens are open to the public. www.squerryes.co.uk (Walk 1)

Chartwell, off Mapleton Road, Westerham, was the home of Sir Winston Churchill and is managed by the National Trust. The stunning views are a key feature of this property which became the Churchill family home. The house includes an unrivalled collection of Churchill paintings and memorabilia while the grounds feature his rose and water gardens. (Walk 1)

Wickhurst Manor, although rebuilt in the 19th century, still contains some of its original structure as an early Wealden hall house and a 15th century doorway has been preserved in the south wall. The manor at Sevenoaks Weald overlooks the Greensand Way.

Riverhill House and gardens lie in the hamlet of Sevenoaks Weald just off the Greensand Way. Azaleas and rhododendrons flourish on the acid Weald soils in the gardens, which were first designed by John Rogers, a founder member of the Royal Horticultural Society, in 1842. Fine trees in the landscaping include acers, cedar, limes, oak and redwood. The house is still family owned and the gardens are open to the public on Sundays and Bank Holidays in Spring and early Summer.

Knole, one of the country's greatest treasure houses, stands in a 1,000-acre deer park – a Site of Special Scientific Interest – near Sevenoaks. Henry VIII liked the house so much that he pressurised his Archbishop of Canterbury, Thomas Cranmer, to give it to him in 1538. It was the birthplace of the novelist and poet Vita Sackville-West and the house, now managed by the National Trust, contains rare collections of Stuart furniture and important portraits by Van Dyck, Gainsborough and Reynolds. (Walk 3)

Ightham Mote is one of The National Trust's most picturesque properties. The moated manor house, which has recently undergone a major conservation project, has an early 14th century great hall, chapel, crypt and two solars. It has

been described as the most complete small medieval manor house in the country. A series of owners have made their impact on this Grade 1 listed building including Edward Haut who enclosed the courtyard and built the range of cottages in the 16th century and Sir Richard Clement who embellished the house with Tudor symbols. (Walk 4)

Fairlawne, at Shipbourne, was bought by Henry Fane who was knighted in 1620 and then took an increasingly active role in politics which led to a great embitterment with Royalty. His son followed in his footsteps after having taken on the estate and supported the Parliamentarian cause in the Civil War. He was executed on Tower Hill in 1662. Over the centuries Fairlawne has thrived and been developed and redeveloped many times. Today it stands in beautiful grounds overlooking well-kept farmland. (Walk 4)

Duke's Place stands on a corner at the east of the village of West Peckham. It was built in the 15th century on land granted by Sir John Culpeper to the Knights Hospitallers of the Order of St John in 1337. The Order was founded during the Crusades to care for the sick and wounded and to look after Christian pilgrims going to Jerusalem.

Thurnham Castle

Roydon Hall, East Peckham, was first built in 1535 and developed by Sir Roger Twysden and his son in the 17th century. Sir Roger was a keen historian and Member of Parliament. Crow-stepped gables and chimneys survive from the early building.

Buston Manor, at Hunton, is an L shaped mansion dating from the late 17th century with fine views to the south. The north wing is said to have medieval origins. The red and blue chequer bricks reflect the wide variety of Wealden clays available.

Linton House, surrounded by Linton Historic Park, replaced an earlier house called Cappell Court dating back to the 14th century. The current stucco house dates from the 1730s with later additions and alterations at the beginning of the 19th century. The 18th century landscape park was redeveloped when the house was enhanced. The village of Linton contains an extensive conservation area and many interesting buildings. (Walk 5)

Boughton Monchelsea Place is a 16th century Kentish ragstone manor house with walled gardens set in 165 acres of wood and parkland. The house, privately owned but available for functions and tours, is set in a dramatic position on the edge of the escarpment. The house, built on the site of a medieval manor house, features Tudor through to Georgian, Gothic and Victorian interiors. The Jacobean galleried staircase, Tudor stone mullioned windows, fireplaces, and Elizabethan and later wall panelling are considered to be of particular note. www.boughtonmonchelseaplace.co.uk (Walk 6)

Sutton Valence School, one of the oldest in the country, was founded by William Lambe in 1576, a wealthy clothmaker. He also built the village almshouses for retired clothworkers and Lambe's house. These still stand in Upper Road but were rebuilt in the 18th and 19th century.

East Sutton Place, now a prison taking in extensive grounds behind 19th century walls, had first been built in the late 16th century. The house was occupied from 1610 by the Filmer family. Sir Robert Filmer was a friend of Charles II and an extreme Royalist. He wrote on the divine right of kings and paid for this when he was besieged in his house by General Fairfax and later imprisoned at Leeds Castle.

Boughton Place is at Boughton Malherbe – one of the smallest villages on the Greensand Way. The attractive ragstone building of today with its mullioned windows is the one surviving wing of a much larger house built in the late 16th century by Sir Edward Wotton. By 1630 it had become one of the most extensive estates in the county set in a deer park. To the south is Coldbridge Farm which incorporates the site of a medieval moated house.

Godinton House, near Ashford, is a Jacobean house with a medieval hall set in 12 acres of restored formal and informal gardens and its park. Many of the rooms of the brick-built house are furnished to reflect the current home's 500-year history. The house was rebuilt incorporating earlier house features for Captain Nicholas Toke, an adventurer who lived 90 years and had five wives, in the 17th century. The more recent Arts and Crafts gardens, designed by Sir Reginald Blomfield, include one of the longest yew hedges in England. Particularly notable are the Rose Garden, Italian and Walled Garden and the delphinium borders.

Godinton Park has been designated as a Local Wildlife Site. The longstanding parkland trees and the pockets of developing woodland provide good nesting opportunities for birds such as the lesser spotted woodpecker.

To find out more about these and other attractions along the Greensand Way, see page 61

along the way

The clearly waymarked Greensand Way starts in the south-west corner of Surrey just 35 miles from London in the market town of Haslemere and runs some 108 miles through the heart of the Kent and Surrey countryside to the cliffs above Romney Marsh.

In addition to farming, people in Haslemere traditionally made their livings from glass making, ironworks and brickmaking. The arrival of the railway in 1859 led to rapid expansion and the town became the centre of the Arts and Crafts Movement.

From Haslemere the path leads to Hindhead Common where Sir Arthur Conan Doyle, the creator of Sherlock Holmes, and the playwright George Bernard Shaw made their homes. Hindhead was a renowned haunt for smugglers and highwaymen and the name of Gibbet Hill recalls the death by hanging of three men accused of murdering a sailor for his purse in the 18th century. A Celtic Cross was erected to mark the spot in 1851. William Cobbet called the place "the most villainous spot God ever made". The views from the Common and Gibbet Hill across the Surrey Hills are outstanding.

The route then follows the route of the old Portsmouth Road, once one of the busiest in England and on to the Devil's Punch Bowl. According to legend the devil hurled a clod of earth at Thor, the god of Thunder, causing a huge hole to appear in the hillside.

Fine farms and historic villages such as Thursley Brook and Witley lead the way along the path up to Hambledon Common. Hambledon is a conservation area with many fine buildings. From Hascombe, the site of an iron age hillfort overlooking the Weald, the Greensand Way leads through the parish of Bramley, across the disused Wey & Arun Canal to Hindhead Common and the spectacular views from Leith Hill with its gothic tower.

Passing along Broadmoor Bottom, where one branch of the River Tilling starts its journey

Ightham

towards the River Wey, the Greensand Way heads through Westcott and Dorking before coming to the conserved landscape of The Nower and Glory Wood through Deepdene and on to Betchworth Park to the village of Brockham, alongside the River Mole, and into Betchworth.

Reigate Park and Reigate Hill lead to the open space of Earlswood Common, once a hive of activity for kilns, claypits and brickmaking, before moving on to South Nutfield and up to Castle Hill below Bletchingley – now an attractive village but once a thriving medieval market town.

From Tandridge, the Greensand Way takes walkers towards the picturesque village of Limpsfield, on the Surrey and Kent border, and High Chart with early glimpses of the North Downs Area of Outstanding Natural Beauty. From Kent Hatch, the Greensand Way passes through Crockham Hill Common and across to Mariners Hill passing near the historic houses at Squerryes Park, Quebec House at Westerham where Sir James Wolfe spent his early years, and Chartwell, which Sir Winston Churchill made his family home from 1922.

Toys Hill marks the highest point in Kent and from here the route heads off to Ide Hill, the parish of Sevenoaks Weald and the grandiose mansion of Knole and its surrounding parkland which stand in sharp contrast to the softer outlines of Ightham Mote and the charming village of Shipbourne.

Now, following the lower slopes of the ridge through arable and pasture, orchards and hop gardens, the Greensand Way passes through the villages of West and East Peckham to the River Medway and on to the lower-lying land between the Medway and the River Beult and the village of Yalding.

From Yalding the route skirts the busy county town of Maidstone and heads towards Hunton, Linton, Boughton Monchelsea and Sutton Valence with their historic houses set in some of the most fertile farmland in the county.

Passing through the traditional villages of East Sutton, Ulcombe and on to Pluckley – the setting for the filming of H. E. Bates''The Darling Buds of May' – the Greensand Way comes into Little Chart in a valley, where the Great Stour opens into

old mill ponds, and on into Hothfield Common nature reserve.

From Hothfield the farming traditions of the county are clear as the path crosses arable and pasture along the lower slopes of the Greensand Ridge through Kingsnorth and on to the national nature reserve at Hamstreet Woods to end the route at the crossroads in the centre of the village of Hamstreet.

Hamstreet has gained national recognition at least twice. It was one of the first areas of England to be mapped by the Ordnance Survey and in 1991 a map of the village appeared on a special edition set of postage stamps marking the bicentenary of the Ordnance Survey.

Great Chart

a fresh approach to
keeping fit

Walking is one of the most pleasurable ways to improve your health, enhance stamina and energy, lower blood pressure and reduce stress.

In addition to the Greensand Way, Kent has a vast range of rural, coastal and town centre walks to suit walkers of all ages and abilities.

As walking requires very little equipment and can be enjoyed throughout the year on your own or with family and friends, it must surely be the most cost-effective and fun way to keep fit.

Ten thousand steps a day are recommended for a healthy lifestyle.

Visit www.kent.gov.uk/explorekent for more information.

Please consult your doctor when undertaking any new physical exercise.

planning your walk

Make sure you have appropriate maps and information about the walk you are planning.

Make a good estimate of how long the walk is likely to take you. Most people average 2 miles (3 kilometres) an hour – steep slopes and rough ground can make the going much slower.

Remember to allow time for rests, refreshment breaks and simply savouring the views.
If you are not used to walking, start with a short walk of 1.5 – 2 miles (2–3 km).

Check the weather forecast for the day. Wear loose-fitting, comfortable and bright clothing appropriate for the season and road walking. Select strong, comfortable shoes with a good gripping sole or walking boots. Sun cream is always advisable but particularly during the Spring and Summer.

Drink plenty of water and take snacks with you.

Carry a mobile phone and let someone else know where you are going and when you expect to return.

If your walk takes you along roads, or across roads, please take care and follow the Highway Code (www.highwaycode.gov.uk).

Signage on Public Rights of Way

Where footpaths, bridleways or byways join a road, a right of way sign (see below) will indicate the route to follow. Additionally, to help people follow a route, waymarkers are installed along a right of way. These are usually coloured arrows fixed or painted onto stiles and gateposts (see below).

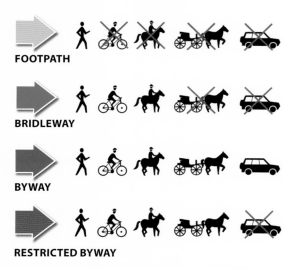

FOOTPATH

BRIDLEWAY

BYWAY

RESTRICTED BYWAY

Signpost

Waymarker

The Countryside Code
Respect – Protect – Enjoy

If you follow the Countryside Code wherever you go, you will enjoy walking in Kent and help protect the countryside now and for future generations.

Be safe, plan ahead and follow any signs. Leave gates and property as you find them.
Protect plants and animals, and take your litter home. Keep dogs under close control.
Consider other people.

Dog walking

The countryside is a great place for dogs to enjoy whether ambling along leafy lanes, rambling through forests, or exploring open access land.

This sign identifies walks in this guidebook that are considered particularly appropriate for dogs.

For further information about the Countryside Code, or copies of 'You and your dog in the countryside', visit **www.countrysideaccess.gov.uk** or phone **0845 100 3298.**

get walking

The following six circular walks are an excellent introduction to the different types of landscape and environment to be enjoyed along the Greensand Way.

Each walk is easy to find with the help of a road map or can be accessed by public transport. You will also find information about where to park, the type and length of the walk and where to enjoy some well earned refreshments.

There is a selection of interesting facts about local history and the many places to be discovered on the walk and nearby. Each walk references the Explorer Map for the area so walkers can also plan their own alternative or extended walks.

There is a 'my journal' page for you to record your own experiences and also details of how to share your interests in a particular walk with other keen walkers.

Once the circular walks have inspired you why not complete the whole Greensand Way. This guidebook provides Explorer Map numbers and Kent Visitor Information centre details to help with the challenge!

Details of further walks across the county are available from www.kent.gov.uk/explorekent.

Please take a few minutes to complete and return the Feedback form at the end of this guidebook. Your feedback will help Kent County Council to develop its range of walking guides.

Wonderfully wild woodland

Take time out to savour the seasonal colours and scents of these hilltop woodlands high above the historic town of Westerham.

26

© Crown copyright 100019238.

Location: Westerham

Distance: 5 miles (8km)

Time: allow 3 hours

Explorer Map: 147

Terrain: Muddy, mainly woodland paths, some steep slopes

Stiles: 11

Parking: Pay & Display at Westerham Town car park

Refreshments and facilities: Westerham town centre, Public House, tearooms, restaurants and shops

Public transport: for information about local bus and train services in Kent, contact Traveline tel: 0871 200 22 33, www.traveline.org.uk

Step count: approx 11,250

The small former market town of Westerham, with its many independent shops, historic public houses, and numerous restaurants and coffee houses is the ideal place to start and finish. This walk takes you high into the hills through peaceful woodland.

As the walk leaves Westerham main road at Lodge Lane and passes a row of lovely cottages you will leave the hustle and bustle of the busy town behind you and begin to enjoy the peace and quite of the Kentish countryside. Take the path on the right to join Mill Lane and then start climbing the hillside.

Open pasture and arable land, with excellent views over rolling hills, historic houses and farms, soon leads into mixed, semi-mature woodland – renowned for its carpet of bluebells in spring, rhododendrons in early Summer, and inspiring colours and sweet chestnuts in Autumn.

The path crosses part of Squerryes Park attached to the famous 17th century manor house. The woodland includes plantations and evidence of coppicing. Leaving the park, the path leads to Goodley Stock and signs of an iron age hillfort can be seen through the trees.

At Kent Hatch turn left from the Link route to join the main Greensand Way. Here majestic, older beech trees can be discovered amid the younger yew, maple, birch and chestnut while the holly gives a colourful touch to darker Winter days.

Patches of deep mud, and at times standing water, along the route indicate the sites of the many springs which feed into the young River Darent above Westerham and add to the diversity of habitats to be found in these woods.

Follow the path steeply downhill turning right past April Cottage and onto the road below. Cross the B2026 to follow the Greensand Way into the woodland of Mariners Hill, which is fast recovering from the widespread damage caused by the fierce winds of the Great Storm in 1987.

The remains of vast uprooted trees and their exposed roots support numerous invertebrates while many mature trees have continued to grow into fascinating forms from their felled trunks. This is a favourite destination for local people and dog walkers seeking a sense of space and tranquillity throughout the year.

Crossing Mapleton Road the path leads alongside the well-tended grounds of Chartwell through mixed woodland. Crossing the lane at the top of the hill, the Greensand Way heads towards French Street, turn left just before reaching the road. You now meander through Hosey Common, which features beech, maple and hornbeam.

After crossing Hosey Common Lane, cross Hosey Common Road and head into Tower Wood with its more formal planting of pines.

As the land slopes down, the path leads once more into open pasture with tremendous views over the valley, Westerham and the North Downs. Open grassland leads to easier walking as the land drops away steeply towards the town and the River Darent.

Sir Winston Churchill was so attached to the home that he had created at Chartwell that he said: "I love the place – a day away from Chartwell is a day wasted."

look out for...

- **Bluebells and rhododendrons in Spring; sweet chestnuts and fungi in Autumn**
- **Moss and lichen**
- **Bats at dusk**
- **A rare 14th century wooden spiral staircase in the tower of St Mary's Church, Westerham**
- **Chartwell, once home to Sir Winston Churchill**

did you know?

Westerham is mentioned in Domesday Book as Oistreham. A colourful Domesday Book celebrating the farming life of the times can be discovered just outside the Westerham Parish Council offices.

In 2004 Robert Wicks established the Westerham Brewery bringing craft brewing back to the town and reviving traditional Kentish real beers. The local hard water, which percolates through the Lower Greensand Ridge to the south of Westerham, is excellent for brewing ales such as the IPA for which Westerham was previously famous.

Old sandstone and ragstone mines at Hosey Common, not open to the public, are now a bat reserve.

Mariners Hill has been owned by the National Trust since 1904. It was one of the first properties to benefit from the protection conferred by the 1907 National Trust Act. The donor was Catherine Southwood Hill, who was one of Octavia Hills' sisters and a founder member of the Trust.

Westerham pond was restored to celebrate the Millennium.

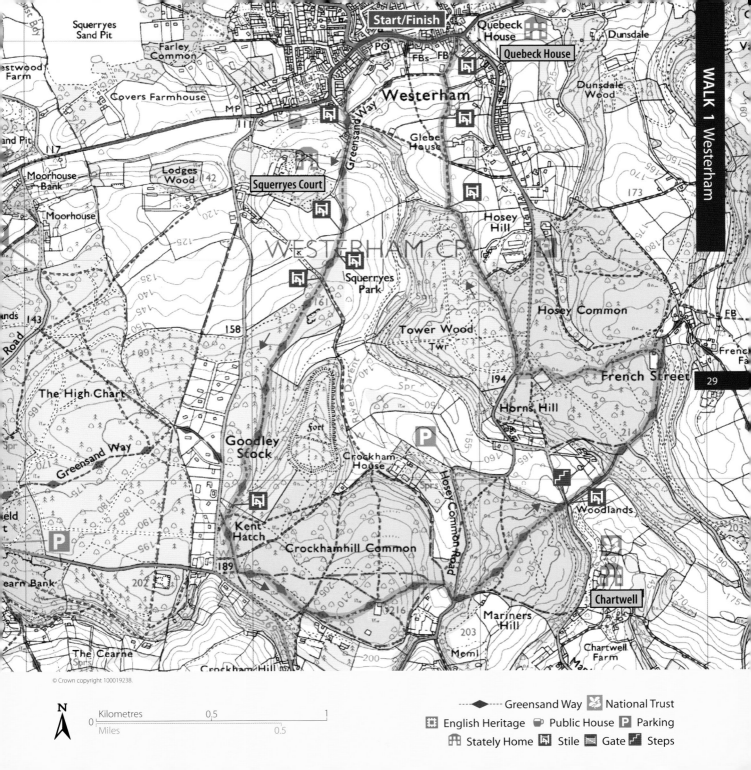

Start/Finish

Quebeck House

Quebeck House

Squerryes Court

Westerham

Glebe House

Hosey Hill

Covers Farmhouse

Squerryes Sand Pit

Farley Common

estwood Farm

Moorhouse Bank

Moorhouse

Lodges Wood

WESTERHAM CR

Squerryes Park

Hosey Common

FB

French Street

173

Tower Wood
Twr

194

Horns Hill

French Fa

29

The High Chart

Greensand Way

fort

Goodley Stock

Crockham House

Sprs

Woodlands

Chartwell

Kent Hatch

Crockhamhill Common

Hosey Common Road

Mariners Hill

Meml

The Cearne

Crockham Hill

Chartwell Farm

eld t

 earn Bank

© Crown copyright 100019238.

N

Kilometres

0   0.5   1

Miles

0.5

- - - ◆ - - - Greensand Way   National Trust

English Heritage   Public House   P Parking

Stately Home   Stile   Gate   Steps

my journal

Date...

I completed the walk in.........................hours and.........................minutes.

My highlights:

This page is for you to record your day exploring the Greensand Way. You may also like to let us know about your experience along the route, recommend a walk or suggest a great day out. Email your comments to **explorekent@kent.gov.uk** with the subject title 'the Greensand Way', or post to: Greensand Way, Environment and Waste, Kent County Council, Invicta House, Maidstone, Kent ME14 1XX.

Peaceful paths and inspiring hills

Even on cold, grey days, it is likely you will encounter fellow walkers also enjoying the peace, quiet and amazing views on this refreshing, popular walk.

Ide hill

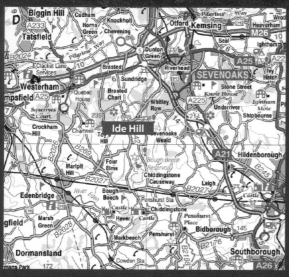

© Crown copyright 100019238.

Location: Ide Hill

Distance: 4 miles (6.4km)

Time: allow 2.5 hours

Explorer Map: 147

Terrain: mainly arable and pasture paths with some roads and some steep slopes

Stiles: 7

Refreshments and facilities: Public house and shop in Ide Hill

Public transport: for information about local bus and train services in Kent, contact Traveline tel: 0871 200 22 33, www.traveline.org.uk

Step count: approx 8,500

Leave the picturesque green at Ide Hill - the highest village in Kent – and follow the path to the first stile to join the Greensand Way and your first taste of the breathtaking panoramic views to be enjoyed along the route.

The path then crosses the bottom of the valley and a gentle brook before heading uphill once again for more views over the Weald.

A bench at the top of the slope offers the opportunity for a rest after the climb. Views such as this inspired Sir Winston Churchill, at home in nearby Chartwell, to declare – "This is what we are fighting for."

Toys Hill, on the right, is maintained by the National Trust and designated as a Site of Special Scientific Interest. This area was an essential part of the local medieval economy for charcoal burners and wood collectors as well as for grazing livestock.

There is still evidence of charcoal pits at Toys Hill but the pits to be found in Scords Wood are mainly from quarrying chert – a stone used in road building.

A chainlink gate leads on up the hillside and into Scords Lane. Follow the path along the valley into open fields mainly used for cattle and arable farming taking advantage of the many small streams that flow across the lower slopes of the Greensand escarpment.

Shielded by woodland and hills on all sides, the route along the valley floor is incredibly peaceful.

A small footbridge leads once more across open farmland before the land begins to rise gently again and pass by historic Henden Manor. Henden Manor Farm covers more than 600 acres and has supported an exceptionally large dairy herd supplying one of the largest UK food retailers.

At the top of the hill head through Chains Farm passing a series of ponds to reach Boar Hill Road and the fringes of the Country Park at Stubbs Wood – a further Site of Special Scientific Interest in this Area of Outstanding Natural Beauty.

English oak and beech trees are the main species to be seen although holly, whitebeam, ash, chestnut, hazel and rowan are also present.

Finally, the hill drops away on the left and you join a road over the ridge crest and follow the path downhill, with fine views across the roofs of the houses set on the hillside.

Rejoin the main highway straight over the crossroads to re-enter Ide Hill. Proceed gently uphill to the green as the road opens out alongside the Cock Inn.

did you know?

The wooden shelter on Ide Hill green is also the village war memorial .

The Victorian church, St Mary the Virgin built around 1865, has an intricate lychgate, crafted by local builder Cecil 'Dusty' Boakes.

During his down-and-out days, George Orwell stayed at the 'spike' in Ide Hill – a temporary home to poor visitors from London helping with the harvest.

Nearby Toy's Hill takes its name from Robert Toys who kept pigs in Otford Woods in the 13th century.

Toy's Hill was once part of the Common of Brasted Chart – locals were permitted to keep their livestock here, gather fuel and quarry Chertstone.

In 1516 Henry VIII gifted Henden Manor to Sir Thomas Boleyn, father of the future Queen Anne. The house you see now is 16th century.

Hanging Bank, towards the end of the walk, is an old gallows site.

At 800 feet above sea level, Ide Hill is one of the highest villages in Kent. In days gone by a beacon was maintained here to transmit alarm signals north to London.

look out for...

- Game birds
- Hedgerow wildlife
- Mature trees
- Songbirds in the undergrowth
- Free range chickens
- Moated grange of Henden Manor
- Carpets of bluebells in Spring; fungi in Autumn
- Breathtaking views

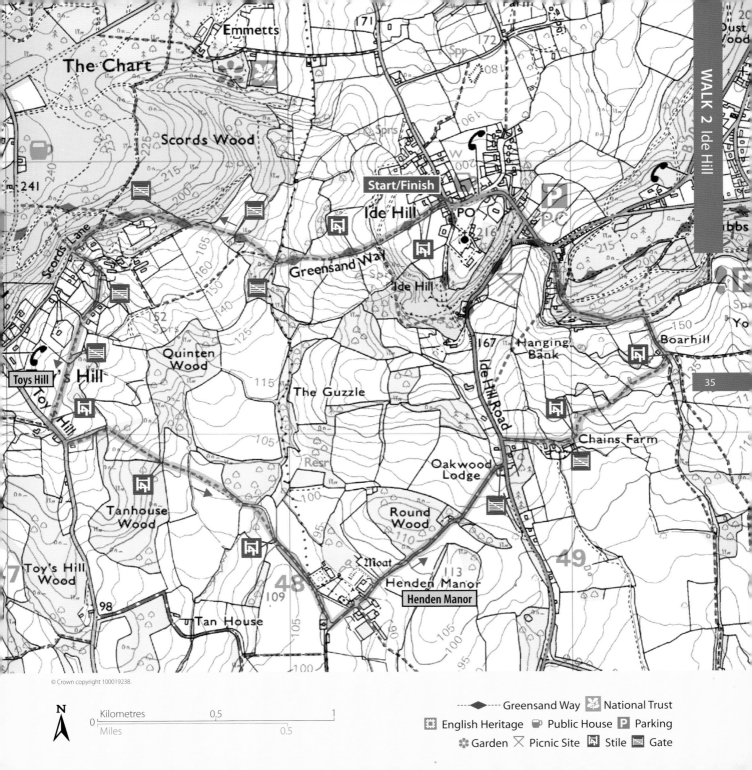

The Chart

Emmetts

Scords Wood

241

Scords Lane

Start/Finish

Ide Hill

PO

216

P

P C

bbs

Greensand Way

Ide Hill

152

Quinten Wood

Toys Hill

'S Hill

The Guzzle

167

Hanging Bank

Boarhill

Yo

35

Tanhouse Wood

Toy's Hill Wood

98

Resr

Oakwood Lodge

Chains Farm

Round Wood

Ide Hill Road

48

109

Moat

Henden Manor

Henden Manor

113

49

Tan House

© Crown copyright 100019238.

N

| Kilometres | | | 0.5 | | | 1 |
| Miles | | | | 0.5 | | |

0

----◆---- Greensand Way   National Trust

English Heritage   Public House   **P** Parking

Garden   Picnic Site   Stile   Gate

my journal

Date...

I completed the walk in..........................hours and................................minutes.

My highlights:

This page is for you to record your day exploring the Greensand Way. You may also like to let us know about your experience along the route, recommend a walk or suggest a great day out. Email your comments to **explorekent@kent.gov.uk** with the subject title 'the Greensand Way', or post to: Greensand Way, Environment and Waste, Kent County Council, Invicta House, Maidstone, Kent ME14 1XX.

Parkland and parakeets

Knole historic deer park, at Sevenoaks, straddles the Greensand Way and is the perfect place for walkers of all ages to enjoy long views across to the North Downs. From here, you can also appreciate the changes of the seasons and wildlife amid historic trees and grasslands.

Knole House

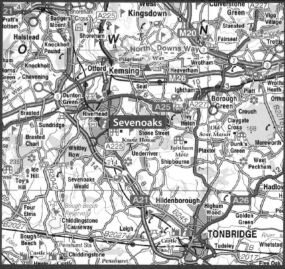

© Crown copyright 100019238.

Location: Sevenoaks

Distance: 4 miles (6.3km)

Time: allow 2 hours

Explorer Map: 147

Terrain: Mainly surfaced paths with some grassed, gentle slopes with one steep slope with handrail

Stiles: 0

Public transport: for information about local bus and train services in Kent, contact Traveline tel: to 0871 200 22 33, www.traveline.org.uk

Step count: approx 8,000

From the Leisure Centre follow the steep path and pass through the metal gate into Knole Park. This is your first chance to glimpse some of the many deer to be seen along the way. It is the only medieval deer park in Kent and one of the very few deer parks to have survived the past 500 years in England. Deer parks for hunting were most popular in the 16th century when the country boasted more than 700.

A former stone ice house serving the big house is clearly visible on your right as you head up the slope and bear off to the right to walk in front of Knole's impressive façade. The path takes you along the old garden walls which are built out of Kentish ragstone.

Wrought-iron gates set in the walls give views in and out of the 24-acre gardens, which include formal and more naturalised plantings. Knole has always been known for its gardens. Archbishop Bourchier established a lavender garden and a small orchard near the house more than 500 years ago.

Leave the stone walls behind to cross the closely-cropped grass and into the open woodland. Elements of the medieval landscape survive here including hawthorn, oak, yew, hornbeam, silver birch, maple and ash – trees that once dominated the Weald.

The flocks of parakeets that make their noisy way overhead are more recent inhabitants of the park which has, in essence, changed little from the early 17th century.

After a short distance, take the path on your right to follow the long, straight Broad Walk. While many landowners set about designing and 'landscaping' their

parks, Knole was left virtually untouched except for the new planting of beech and broad tree-lined avenues replacing some of the older coppiced woodlands.

Towards the end of the Broad Walk, turn left down the Chestnut Walk with its ancient avenue of trees where sweet chestnuts and rich golden leaves scatter the path in Autumn. Newer plantings are closely fenced as protection from the deer.

While the Greensand Way turns off to the left, continue straight and follow the path to head gently downhill through the open woodland. Pass the pond by Keepers Cottage on your left and across the golf course. From the higher points there are long views across the valley to the chalk Downs beyond.

The National Trust tea rooms, set in a stone courtyard at the back of the main house, offer a warm welcome and the opportunity for a short break before rejoining the path across the grasslands to return to the car park.

Numerous paths, including a bridleway, cross Knole Park, and there are many opportunities to take diversions to extend or shorten a circular walk through this popular and peaceful landscape.

did you know?

Henry VIII liked Knole so much that he persuaded Thomas Cranmer, Archbishop of Canterbury, to give it to him in 1538. Not everyone has been so impressed by the house. The 17th century diarist John Evelyn was depressed by the greyness of this "great old fashion'd house" and went outside to escape into the sunshine.

Knole deer park, which covers 1,000 acres, is designated as a Site of Special Scientific Interest.

Thomas Sackville converted the late medieval Archbishop's Palace into a Renaissance mansion in the early 17th century.

Knole is the birthplace of the novelist and poet Vita Sackville-West. She wrote of the great house: "It has the tone of England; it melts into the green of the garden turf, into the tawnier green of the park beyond, into the blue of the pale English sky."

The Sackville family gave Knole to the National Trust in 1946 with an endowment for its maintenance.

look out for...

- Deer
- Birds including parakeets
- Ice house
- Kentish ragstone
- Sweet chestnuts
- Views of the North Downs

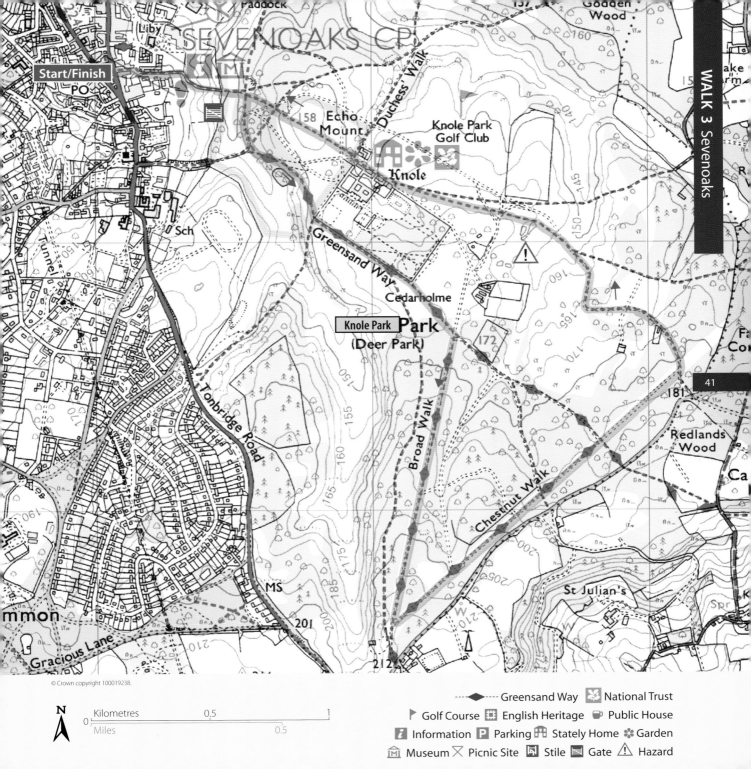

Start/Finish
PO

SEVENOAKS C.P.
Liby
Paddock

Echo
Mount
158

Duchess' Walk

Knole Park
Golf Club

Knole

Sch

Greensand Way

Cedarholme

Knole Park Park
(Deer Park)

172

Tonbridge Road

Tunnel

Broad Walk

Chestnut Walk

Redlands
Wood

St Julian's

MS
201

Gracious Lane

mmon

Godden
Wood

41

181

Fa
Co

Ca

© Crown copyright 100019238.

N

Kilometres
0   0.5   1
Miles
0.5

- - -◆- - - Greensand Way   National Trust
▶ Golf Course   English Heritage   Public House
ℹ Information   P Parking   Stately Home   Garden
Museum   ✕ Picnic Site   Stile   Gate   ⚠ Hazard

my journal

Date ....

I completed the walk in .... hours and .... minutes.

My highlights:

This page is for you to record your day exploring the Greensand Way. You may also like to let us know about your experience along the route, recommend a walk or suggest a great day out. Email your comments to **explorekent@kent.gov.uk** with the subject title 'the Greensand Way', or post to: Greensand Way, Environment and Waste, Kent County Council, Invicta House, Maidstone, Kent ME14 1XX.

As pretty as a picture

Discover this enchanting stroll through classic Kentish
countryside and peaceful Plaxtol.

Shipbourne Village Green

44

St Giles' Church

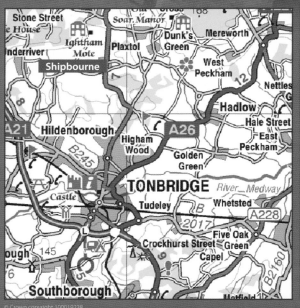

© Crown copyright 100019238.

Location: Shipbourne

Distance: 5 miles (8km)

Time: allow 3 hours

Explorer Map: 147

Terrain: Fields and roads, some moderate slopes

Stiles: 14

Parking: available at The Common in Shipbourne. (Please park considerately)

Refreshments and facilities: Chaser Inn Shipbourne, Kentish Rifleman Dunts Green

Public transport: for information about local bus and train services in Kent, contact Traveline tel: to 0871 200 22 33, www.traveline.org.uk

Step count: approx 10,500

Majestic trees, rolling open fields, historic houses and the picturesque village of Plaxtol – one of the most scenic areas in Kent – make this peaceful Greensand Way walk a delight for all the family throughout the year.

From Shipbourne, head along the path by St Giles' Church and through the kissing gate out into the open fields. Follow the path at the edge of the field alongside the Fairlawne Estate cricket ground and past pasture fields that in Springtime are home to flocks of sheep. At the end of the footpath bear left to follow the bridleway. At this point you may wish to take a diversion to take in views of Ightam Mote, one of the finest examples of a medieval house conserved by the National Trust.

Our route however continues uphill towards Ivy Hatch through Scathes Wood.

At the top of the hill, cross the A227 to follow the bridleway along High Beeches. At the end of the woodland you will enjoy some excellent views of the surrounding area to the south before heading downhill towards Plaxtol Lane.

Come into the village turning right along Plaxtol Lane passing the church and right again by the village war memorial and the fine yew topiary at Church House. The Street features attractive traditional cottages and the popular Papermakers Arms – a reminder of one of the area's most important industries in the past.

Many Plaxtol houses date from the 14th and 15th centuries are still private homes at the heart of this thriving village community with its long history. A small Roman corridor villa, with a bath house, was discovered to the south east of the village in the 19th century and excavations uncovered a bronze statuette of Minerva.

From the village, follow the route back into open pasture and along the quiet banks of the River Bourne and on to pass a roadside nature reserve and the Kentish Rifleman public house which dates from the mid 17th century.

From Dunks Farm Road, a gate leads into fields with a classic Kent orchard on the right. The slight climb is rewarded by fine views over mature woodland and beyond. Cross School Lane and pass through the grounds of Fairlawne Home Farm to a bridge over the stream.

The route then passes through a kissing gate and alongside village houses to return to Shipbourne Common.

Sir Henry Vane the Younger's body lies in the crypt of Shipbourne Church in a stone coffin that, due to his beheading, is noticeably shorter than all the others. Sir Henry Vane was a Royalist, then became a Roundhead and then switched back to being a Royalist under Charles I. He was executed as it was thought that he was too dangerous to live. His ghost is said to wander the village.

did you know?

A farmers' market featuring fine local produce is held at St Giles' Church, Shipbourne, every Thursday morning. Stallholders pay a small fee each week to cover costs and this is donated to charities. The market gives more than £3,000 to charity each year.

St Giles' Church at Shipbourne was built by Sir Edward Cazelete, of Fairlawne, in the 19th century but in the 15th century a chapel on this site originally belonged to the Knights Hospitaller of St John.

Plaxtol Church has no dedication to a patron saint because it was built in 1649 in the time of Oliver Cromwell. It is thought to have replaced an ancient chapel on the Roman way from Lympne to London.

Hyders Forge, Plaxtol, is now a housing area but was once the site of a busy forge and an important employer in the village.

look out for...

- The historic homes of Ightham Mote and Fairlawne
- Mature woodland
- The original oak Cromwellian altar in the Lady Chapel at Plaxtol Church
- The old village pound where lost animals of the village were locked up at night by the high wall on the north side of Plaxtol Churchyard
- A roadside nature reserve

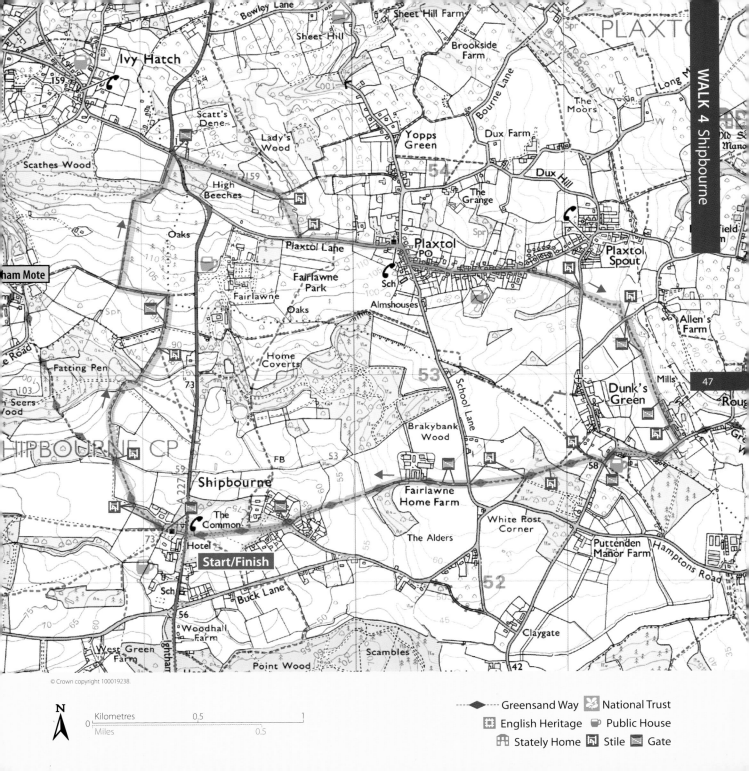

© Crown copyright 100019238.

47

Ivy Hatch

Sheet Hill Farm

Bewley Lane

Sheet Hill

Brookside Farm

PLAXTO

River Bourne

Long M

The Moors

Scatt's Dene

Lady's Wood

Bourne Lane

Yopps Green

Dux Farm

Dux Hill

Scathes Wood

High Beeches

Old S
Mano

The Grange

Oaks

Plaxtol Lane

Plaxtol
PO

Plaxtol Spout

ham Mote

Fairlawne Park

Sch

Allen's Farm

Fairlawne

Oaks

Almshouses

Home Coverts

53

Fatting Pen

Mills

Dunk's Green

Rou

Seers Wood

School Lane

Brakybank Wood

58

HIPBOURNE CP

Shipbourne

FB

Fairlawne Home Farm

White Rost Corner

The Common

The Alders

Puttenden Manor Farm

Hotel

Hamptons Road

Start/Finish

Sch

Buck Lane

52

Woodhall Farm

Claygate

West Green Farm

Point Wood

Scambles

42

N

Kilometres
0   0.5   1

Miles
0   0.5

······◆····· Greensand Way   National Trust

English Heritage   Public House

Stately Home   Stile   Gate

my journal

Date ....

I completed the walk in .... hours and .... minutes.

My highlights:

This page is for you to record your day exploring the Greensand Way. You may also like to let us know about your experience along the route, recommend a walk or suggest a great day out. Email your comments to **explorekent@kent.gov.uk** with the subject title 'the Greensand Way', or post to: Greensand Way, Environment and Waste, Kent County Council, Invicta House, Maidstone, Kent ME14 1XX.

Orchards and oasts – a taste of the Garden of England

Open parkland, orchards, oasts and incredible panoramic views over the Weald to the South Downs make this a truly memorable walk.

Linton Village

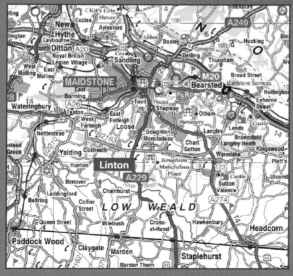

© Crown copyright 100019238.

Location: Linton

Distance: 4 miles (6.4km)

Time: allow 2.5 hours

Explorer Map: 136, 148

Terrain: mainly arable and pastures paths with some road sections

Stiles: 8

Steps: 2 sets

Public transport: for information about local bus and train services in Kent, contact Traveline tel: 0871 200 22 33, www.traveline.org.uk

Step count: approx 8,400

Start in the centre of the small and enchanting village of Linton, on the outskirts of Maidstone, with its typically Kentish church, neighbouring almshouses and village inn – The Bull – owned by Shepherd Neame, Britain's oldest brewer.

Walk through the churchyard and out of the gate into the parkland beyond to join the Greensand Way and follow the ridge high above the River Beult. The impressive white walls of Linton House can be glimpsed through the trees on the right as the path passes through light woodland and copses of holly, sycamore and sweet chestnut.

Cross Loddington Lane to walk alongside well established orchards – a mass of blossom in Spring and richly apple-scented in Autumn, high hedges help protect the fruit trees from potentially damaging winds. Gradually the fine views across to the right open up towards Goudhurst.

Even clearer dramatic views can be enjoyed from alongside St Peters' Church, Boughton Monchelsea. The lychgate is thought to date from the 15th century and is possibly the oldest in Kent.

Walk up the hill alongside the weathered walls of Boughton Monchelsea Place with their rich mosses and lichens and on through the car park and out again into the fields – some of which are used for pasture while others take advantage of the good local soils for arable crops.

Here the circular walk leaves the Greensand Way skirting round the end of the large deer park through more orchards, alongside a former quarry and then heads steeply downhill. Fast streams can run down these slopes after prolonged wet weather and planks have been put across the ditches to assist walkers wishing to keep their feet dry.

Cattle and sheep flourish in these luxurious fields. Follow the marked route across the fields dotted with mature, specimen trees through to join the quiet country lane and on to Church Hill. Turn left and rejoin the route on the right to pass through further orchards, farmland and coppiced woodland.

Crossing the small bridge and stile turn left into Loddington Lane and follow the road turning off to the right at the first footpath sign into the heart of Linton Park. Look to the right for views of the impressive white Palladian mansion with its high flagpole. Continue to cross the park to reach the lake on your left – filled with water lillies and a popular habitat for waterfowl throughout the Summer.

Finally leave the park behind to reach Linton Hill. Turn right up the hill and back to the car park opposite The Bull.

St Peter's Church, at Boughton Monchelsea, was seriously damaged by fire in 1832 while St Nicholas Church, at Linton, was struck by lightning in 1838. Part of the spire was destroyed.

look out for...

- **Almshouses**
- **Apple orchards**
- **Linton House**
- **Lychgate at Boughton Monchelsea**
- **Oast houses**
- **Livestock**
- **Unusual tombstones at St Peter's Church**

did you know?

Stone has been quarried for building from the Greensand Ridge here since Roman times. The last quarry closed in the 1960s.

The oldest part of The Bull at Linton is believed to date from the 16th century and was built as a watering hole for travellers. The pub is reputed to be haunted and there are tales of secret tunnels.

Apples originated in the Middle East more than 4,000 years ago. They probably came to the UK with the Romans but it was really in the Norman era that specially cultivated varieties spread across Europe. Apple growing was in decline in England following the Black Death and the Wars of the Roses. Orchards were revived by Henry VIII who instructed his fruiterer to scour the known world for the best varieties which he planted in Kent.

Apple pips contain traces of cyanide but not enough to be harmful.

Fallow deer have wandered in Boughton Monchelsea Place deer park for more than 300 years.

Linton House was built in the 1730s on the site of Capell Court. The house served as the headquarters in 1778 – 9 for more than 11,000 soldiers camping out between Coxheath and Boughton Monchelsea ready to repel a French invasion.

Lyewood Farm
Court
Green Lane
Brisling Lane
W
Boughton Monchelsea
Haste Hill
PO
Monchelsea Fm
Wr Twr
B 2163
Sch
Heath Road
108
Cock Street
M
Hill Farm
Sch
Parsonage Farm
Tilt's Wood
76
Resr
BS
BS
Earthwork
117
77
78
Linton Park
Loddington Farm
BS
Earthwork
Start/Finish
P
Home Farm
Linton
83
The White Lodge
Boughton Monchelsea Place
Wierton Place
Linton Park
BSs
Deer Park
MS
LINTON C
Mon
53
Linton
Church Farm
52
East Hal
47
Linton Park
BOUGHTON MONCHELSEA
Loddington Lane
Brick Kiln Wood
Ppg Sta
Resr
31
Gravitt Cottage
Redwall Farm
Butt Green Lane
34
BS
Darnold Wood
27
Bishop's Farm
Rankins Farm
32
Ranter's Plantation
BSs
BS
River Wood
Linton Hill
bridge Lane
18
Her
Long Lane
30

© Crown copyright 100019238.

N

Kilometres		
0	0.5	1
Miles		
	0.5	

◆--- Greensand Way   🌿 National Trust
🏛 English Heritage   🍺 Public House
🏰 Stately Home   🔲 Stile   ▥ Gate   ⌁ Steps

my journal

Date ....

I completed the walk in .... hours and .... minutes.

My highlights:

This page is for you to record your day exploring the Greensand Way. You may also like to let us know about your experience along the route, recommend a walk or suggest a great day out. Email your comments to **explorekent@kent.gov.uk** with the subject title 'the Greensand Way', or post to: Greensand Way, Environment and Waste, Kent County Council, Invicta House, Maidstone, Kent ME14 1XX.

Fertile farms in the heart of Kent

A bright sunny day is perfect for enjoying the rich and fertile Kent countryside and outstanding views across the valley of the Great Stour to the North Downs. This circular walk starts in the historic grounds of St James' Church in the rural village of Egerton.

Egerton

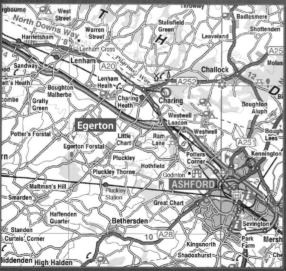

© Crown copyright 100019238.

Location: Egerton, near Ashford

Distance: 3.1 miles (5km)

Time: allow 2 hours

Explorer Map: 137

Terrain: Paths mainly cross arable and pasture fields

Stiles: 8

Public transport: for information about local bus and train services in Kent, contact Traveline tel: 0871 200 22 33, www.traveline.org.uk

Step count: approx 6,510

Farming is still key to the economy of this area of Kent and its many small villages. Along the route old and more recently planted apple orchards stand alongside extensive arable fields while cattle and sheep graze the slopes of the Greensand Ridge.

Follow the waymarked Greensand Way through the gate from the churchyard and into the apple orchards with their spectacular displays of blossom in Spring and plentiful harvests of fruit in Autumn. Head alongside the tall stone walls surrounding Egerton House and through the gate, passing Foxden Lodge on the right. Early views across the Great Stour open out to the right.

Cross over the road and into the fields where the land begins to fall away gradually and springs make the earth soft underfoot. Small areas of woodland shield the fields and crops from crosswinds breaking up the landscape as the Greensand Way heads across small streams.

At the junction turn left along the byway leaving the Greensand Way and continue downhill along the edge of Coldbridge Wood. At the end of the surfaced track you reach a gate, pass through this gate and follow the field edge marked with wooden posts to reach a crossroads with a footpath. From here you head south west towards the fingerpost at the far side of the pasture field.

The route then crosses Egerton House Road to head uphill along the footpath directly opposite. Continue along this path following the hedgeline on your left untill reaching a stile. After crossing the stile continue ahead to reach Link Hill Lane next to Link Cottage.

At Link Hill Lane turn left and take the path directly ahead up the steps and into the arable field.

The route passes along the edge of the field with the tower of St James' in Egerton clearly visible. Take the path alongside the village school and the stone steps down to the road in the centre of the village.

Egerton is home to many listed properties such as Egerton House, St. James' Church and a Tumulus, which is a Bronze Age burial ground.

look out for...

- **Stained glass and Darell Monuments, St James' Church, Egerton**
- **Orchards**
- **Pheasants**
- **Cattle**
- **Sheep**
- **Horses**
- **Arable crops**
- **Beacon at Boughton Malherbe**

did you know?

Egerton Village Store and Post Office stocks a wide range of Kent produce including Egerton cookies, jams made at nearby Wye and Pluckley tea.

There is a tomb to Sir John Darell who served Henry VII in St James' Church, Egerton. Sir John died in 1509.

The chandelier in St James' Church is lit by 36 candles.

The flagpole outside St Nicholas Church, Boughton Malherbe, was erected to mark the Millennium.

Queen Elizabeth 1 visited Bocton Hall, now Boughton Place.

Legend claims that the Old Rectory, at Boughton Malherbe, was haunted by the ghost of a monk. It is said that a former rector used to offer lodgings to passing tramps just to test the reputation of the house's haunted room. No-one is thought to have stayed in the room for more than an hour or two.

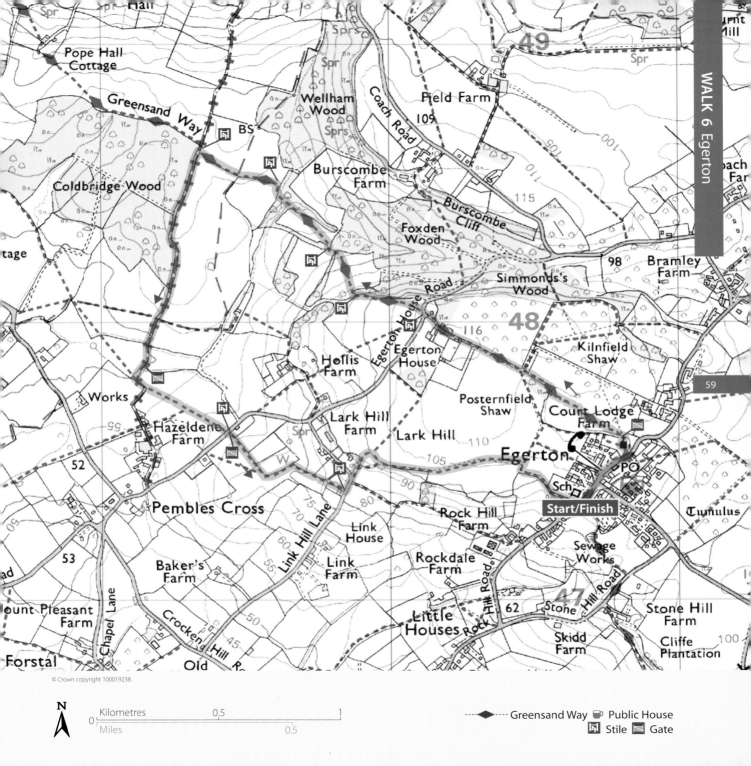

49

Spr

Pope Hall
Cottage

Greensand Way

BS

Coldbridge Wood

Wellham
Wood

Sprs

Field Farm
109

Coach Road

Burscombe
Farm

Burscombe
Cliff

115

98

Bramley
Farm

Foxden
Wood

Simmonds's
Wood

48

116

Egerton House Road

Hollis
Farm

Egerton
House

Kilnfield
Shaw

59

Works

Hazeldene
Farm

52

Lark Hill
Farm

Spr

W

Lark Hill

Posternfield
Shaw

110

Court Lodge
Farm

Egerton

PO

Sch

105

Start/Finish

Pembles Cross

Link
House

90

Rock Hill
Farm

Tumulus

53

Baker's
Farm

Link Hill Lane

Link
Farm

Rockdale
Farm

Sewage
Works

50

Mount Pleasant
Farm

Chapel Lane

Crockenhill Road

Old

Little
Houses

Rock Hill Road

47

62

Stone

Skidd
Farm

Stone Hill
Farm

Cliffe
Plantation

Forstal

© Crown copyright 100019238.

N

Kilometres
0   0.5   1
Miles
0.5

◆ Greensand Way   ⌑ Public House
🔲 Stile   ▦ Gate

my journal

Date...

I completed the walk in........................hours and........................minutes.

My highlights:

This page is for you to record your day exploring the Greensand Way. You may also like to let us know about your experience along the route, recommend a walk or suggest a great day out. Email your comments to **explorekent@kent.gov.uk** with the subject title 'the Greensand Way', or post to: Greensand Way, Environment and Waste, Kent County Council, Invicta House, Maidstone, Kent ME14 1XX.

Attractions on the Greensand Way

Further information

Visit www.visitkent.co.uk and www.visitsoutheastengland.com for information about visitor attractions, places to stay and events throughout the year.

Details of National Trust properties and sites along the Greensand Way are available at www.nationaltrust.org.uk. Natural England site wildlife and conservation information can be found at www.naturalengland.org.uk

For more walking experiences in Kent visit Explore Kent at www.kent.gov.uk/explorekent

Local Visitor Information Centres

KENT

Ashford Visitor Information Centre
18 The Churchyard, Ashford, Kent
tel: 01233 629165
email: tourism@ashford.gov.uk
www.ashford.gov.uk

Broadstairs Visitor Information Centre
tel: 0870 264 6111
email: tourism@thanet.gov.uk
www.visitthanet.co.uk

Canterbury Visitor Information Centre
tel: 01227 378100
email: canterburyinformation@canterbury.gov.uk
www.canterbury.gov.uk

Deal Visitor Information Centre
tel: 01304 369576

Dover Visitor Information Centre
tel: 01304 205108
email: tic@doveruk.com
www.whitecliffscountry.com

Faversham Visitor Information Centre
tel: 01795 534542
email: ticfaversham@btconnect.com
www.faversham.org

Gravesend Visitor Information Centre
tel: 01474 337600
email: info@towncentric.co.uk
www.towncentric.co.uk

Herne Bay Visitor Information Centre
tel: 01227 361911
email: hernebayinformation@canterbury.gov.uk
www.visithernebay.co.uk

Maidstone Visitor Information Centre
tel: 01622 602169
email: tourism@maidstone.gov.uk
www.tour-maidstone.co.uk

Margate Visitor Information Centre
tel: 0870 264 6111
email: tourism@thanet.gov.uk
www.visitthanet.co.uk

Ramsgate Visitor Information Centre
tel: 0870 264 6111
email: tourism@thanet.gov.uk
www.visitthanet.co.uk

Rochester Visitor Information Centre
tel: 01634 843666
email: visitor.centre@medway.gov.uk
www.medway.gov.uk

Sevenoaks Visitor Information Centre
tel: 01732 450305
email: tic@sevenoakstown.org.uk
www.heartofkent.org.uk

Swanley Visitor Information Centre
tel: 01322 614660
email: tourisminfo@swanley.org.uk

Tonbridge Visitor Information Centre
tel: 01732 770929
email: tonbridge.castle@tmbc.gov.uk
www.heartofkent.org.uk

Tunbridge Wells Visitor Information Centre
tel: 01892 515675
email: touristinformationcentre@tunbridgewells.co.uk
www.heartofkent.org.uk

Weald Information Centre
tel: 01580 715686

SURREY
Guildford Tourist Information Centre
tel: 01483 444333
email: tic@guildford.gov.uk
www.guildford.gov.uk

Woking Visitor Information Centre
tel: 01483 720103
email: tourist@woking.gov.uk
www.woking.gov.uk

Haslemere Visitor Information Centre
tel: 01428 645425
email: vic@haslemere.com
www.haslemere.com

Dorking Visitor Information Centre
tel: 01306 879327
email: visitor.information@mole-valley.gov.uk
www.mole-valley.gov.uk

Your Feedback

Thank you for buying Kent County Council's Greensand Way guidebook. We hope you enjoy reading it and have fun exploring the length of the river and the surrounding chalk hills. We really appreciate feedback from our customers and use it to develop the right services and products for you. Please take a few minutes to complete and return this form.

How did you find out about the Greensand Way guidebook?

- [ ] Explore Kent website
- [ ] 'word of mouth'
- [ ] browsing in a shop
- [ ] Visitor Information Centre

Other

Were you given the guidebook as a gift or did you buy it?

Where did you buy your copy of this guidebook?

What do you like most about this guidebook?

What do you like least about this guidebook?

How would you rate the guidebook between 1 & 5
1 (poor) - 5 (excellent)

[ ]	[ ]	[ ]	[ ]	[ ]
1	2	3	4	5

About you

- [ ] Male [ ] Female

Age
- [ ] under 18 years
- [ ] 18 - 29
- [ ] 30 - 39
- [ ] 40 - 49
- [ ] 50 - 59
- [ ] 60 - 69
- [ ] Over 69

Are you a visitor to or resident of Kent?

- [ ] Visitor [ ] Resident

Any further comments

Please tear out and send your feedback to:-
Environment and Waste, Kent County Council,
Invicta House, Maidstone, Kent ME14 1XX

Thank you for your time.
If you would like to be kept up to date with Explore Kent products please tick the box and write your name and address or your email address below. [ ]

🔒 We'd like to keep you posted on Explore Kent news. Don't worry, we will not overload you with post or emails and we will not pass on or sell any personal information you share with us.